Raspberry Pi 2

The Essential Step by Step beginner's User guide to mastering a full list of projects for the Raspberry Pi 2

Introduction

I want to thank you and congratulate you for downloading the book, *"Raspberry Pi 2: The Essential Step by Step beginner's User guide to mastering a full list of projects for the Raspberry Pi 2"*.

This book contains proven steps and strategies on how to start your Raspberry Pi 2 project.

Nowadays, many people have been trying to dabble with computing and robotics. They want to make their own system using PCBs and technological setups right at home. This is now possible with the availability of mini computing systems like Raspberry Pi 2.

This book will teach you all the vital knowledge to know about Raspberry Pi 2. Knowledge you'll learn are about the hardware and its components. You'll know each part's functions. It is among the basics that everyone who's new in Raspberry Pi 2 must know.

Aside from the hardware, you'll also learn about the software used for using the PCB. It requires programming to execute functions. You'll also learn how both Raspberry hardware and software work together and coding basics that you'll need.

Finally, you'll get to know more tips and reminders about this platform and projects suitable for beginners.

Thanks again for downloading this book, I hope you enjoy it!

Chapter 1
Introduction to Raspberry Pi 2

High technology systems developed today are becoming more accessible for regular consumers through solutions like Raspberry Pi. Before trying Raspberry Pi 2, you must learn vital introductions about this PCB. In this chapter, you'll learn:

- The short history of Raspberry Pi and Pi 2

- The goals behind launching and distributing this system.

- The hardware and the software versions

- Available Raspberry Pi models

- And advantages in learning the Raspberry Pi

From Raspberry Pi

Raspberry Pi 2's predecessor is Raspberry Pi, a small, single-board computer developed in United Kingdom. Named after its manufacturing group, the Raspberry Pi Foundation, Raspberry Pi is loaded with components found in a regular computer motherboard compressed in small package.

The group behind the Raspberry Pi conceptualized its architecture based on an Atmel microcontroller, the integrated circuit serving as brain for small form factor circuit boards. They came up with a board that utilizes components that can be manipulated or designed according to what developers want to produce. These experts took advantage of cheaper mobile device parts, which became prominent in 2008, to improve their concept board. During this time, processors for Mobil devices have been enhanced to improve new portable devices users produced in the same year. Through these improved components, the developers came up with several prototypes of their hand-made Raspberry Pi. After several pre-launch production and auction, Raspberry Pi started to roll out in February 2012, with reports of buyers receiving their new boards in April of the same year. Several models of Raspberry Pis were released in the market with varying specifications.

After three years, the Raspberry Pi Foundation announced the upcoming new Raspberry Pi called Raspberry Pi 2 (RPi2). Also known as Raspberry Pi model B, the newest computer board hit the market with 1 GB of RAM and support for Windows 10, the latest OS upgrade rolled out by Microsoft. Considering the positive ratings received by its predecessors, the developer and techy individuals have high expectations of Raspberry Pi 2. You'll learn more about its hardware components later.

Goal in Using Raspberry Pi 2

The declining computer skill level among individuals taking Computer Science in 2006 prompted the Raspberry Pi Foundation to produce this product. According to the brains behind this project, the 1990s era of Computer Science hopefuls is a time with a lot of individuals who are dabbling with computing themselves. They are serious hobbyists who built their own devices, which gave them an edge in competing as Computer Science experts. By 2000, skill levels of Computer Science applicants noticeably declined. The developers aimed to use this device to promote in-school basic computer education, especially for those aiming to enter the Computer Science industry. Many schools began to use the product to promote early computer education for students.

Although not highlighted on their official website, the Raspberry Pi Foundation somehow produced a product that can inspire individuals who are planning to work in the field. Most of the time, computer programmers and technicians need to have a taste of what they'll do once they made it to the real computer science world.

Finally, the company aimed to promote computer science education without spending a fortune. During its production period, the Foundation thought of distributing this product in two models: one costing $25 and $35 for the second version. Raspberry Pi 2 is offered at $35, which means buyers can take advantage of its enhance features at the same price as the earlier Raspberry Pi releases.

Advantages of Learning Raspberry Pi 2

As for the advantages, being able to but their hands on a high tech component lets an individual be more inspired in pursuing the industry and even introducing it to other individuals who are looking for a lucrative field to venture.

Aside from having a taste of the industry, being experienced in manipulating this device prepares students to the field. They will be more confident on their skills and add up their newly acquired knowledge to be a better programmer and technician in the future.

Raspberry Pi Hardware and Software

Raspberry Pi 2 comes in two versions—the hardware and the software version. The hardware version is the board that can be purchased from the foundation's website or authorized distributors. They distribute them to people worldwide and sold in dollars.

After getting the hardware, users must download Raspberry Pi's software to load programs and manipulate the system. Several software distributions are available and can be downloaded from the foundation's website. It runs in special programming codes, which will be useful in utilizing the board for making the project. You'll know more about the software aspect of this product on Chapter 3.

Models

The earlier Raspberry Pi came in four models. This four generation utilized the same graphic processor unit (GPU), central processing unit (CPU) and system on a chip (SoC). Their differences are their video and audio outputs, memory capacity, on board storage, on-board storage, and peripherals.

As the newest release, Raspberry Pi 2 comes with better features than its predecessors due to completely developed portable device technology that can support multitasking for RPi2 projects. Since you want to only learn about Raspberry Pi 2, this will be the main focus in the book instead of discussing the earlier models in detail.

Chapter 2
A Look at the Hardware

Carrying out an effective and flawless Raspberry Pi 2 project is about knowing the hardware and the software. The hardware helps developers to apply safe and key procedures that will run the system and see the needed output. in this section, you'll learn about:

- Raspberry Pi 2's parts and their functions

- Additional accessories that will be useful for programs

Identifying Parts

If you've seen a computer motherboard, you'll find the same components in Raspberry Pi 2 although they are arranged on a small circuit board instead on a large board. Knowing its components will teach you their functions and procedure application and proper care. Raspberry Pi 2 comes with the following components:

Processor

The processor or CPU serves as the board's bring for processing information and generating data. It aids in ensuring data transfer within the system works smoothly. This new model has the highest recorded processor capacity among Raspberry Pi models at 900 MHz ARM Cortex-A7 quad-core. This CPU capacity is sufficient in enabling Pi 2 to handle multitasking within the system and ensure projects will run properly.

RAM

RAM or random access memory has been supercharged in this model. It has 1 GB memory, which is 50 percent higher than its predecessor's, Raspberry Pi Model B+, memory capacity. Nowadays, some computers still run on 1GB memory, and it contributes to speedy performance given that the operated programs don't require extreme amount of resources.

SoC

Also known as integrated circuit, system on chip (SoC) is a component that contains a variety of signals exchanged within the system. This component is widely used in this type of board due to its lower power usage, which is similar to some portable devices. Raspberry Pi 2's SoC is Broadcom BCM 2836.

USB Ports

Although the system is already cramped up with components, this credit card-sized module has four USB ports for data transfer during programming, which is two times more than its predecessor.

Audio Out

Audio out is a port for sounds, which is commonly used for many projects. Users will have a multimedia experience on a small chip with this system.

SD Card Slot

SD card slot is for placing SD memory card containing a program image. This image will be used as a preliminary operating system for Raspberry Pi projects. It can be enhanced to support various tasks. Today, the program that comes with Raspberry Pi 2 has special setup that prepares SD cards for copying unzipped files. A large-capacity memory card will be formatted to FAT storage type like 4 GB memory cards and higher. Once the files are expanded and copied, the system will be rebooted and users can select from six operating systems for installation according to their personal preference or special requirements.

Ethernet Port

The availability of Ethernet port sets Raspberry Pi 2 above its predecessors. The earlier ones didn't have this feature, which kept earlier developers from taking advantage of the internet for their projects. Nowadays, this additional allows users to explore and integrate internet connection and even media screening.

Camera Interface

It supports a camera interface that underwent numerous enhancements due to some issues with Xenon flash on some project. You'll learn more about this flash problem in the last chapter.

HDMI Port

The addition of HDMI port brings Raspberry Pi 2 to the next multimedia level. HDMI port utilizes digital signals that ensure faster data transfer between the input and output video ports. Developers can use this feature in creating the finest programming system for multimedia. Considering the processor, memory, system chip and its graphic cards, Raspberry Pi 2 can withstand the demand of digital data transfer that will improve their projects.

Graphics Core

The graphics processing unit is Broadcom VideoCore IV running at 250 MHz, which is also a high speed graphics chip that supports high definition media decoders and encoders.

GPIO

GPIO means General Purpose Input/Output is a programmable generic pin through a program. Through programming, this component can work with input and output pin. GPIO is a group of pins look like an IDE slot in typical computer motherboard. Exposing these input/output pins let installed peripherals use the CPU.

Accessories

Several accessories can be installed with the system to make specific projects work. They can be purchased with the system or from trusted distributors found online. Common accessories purchased with this board are cameras and WiFi adapters.

Cameras

The Foundation presented two types of cameras that can be used with the system. First is the typical camera launched with Raspberry Pi paired with a firmware update to make sure the system will function. It comes with accessories like flexible flat cable. Its supported resolutions start at 640x480p up to 1080p, which means this camera will work with HDMI system for output after taking the photos or videos.

WiFi Adapters

WiFi adapters let developers connect their boards in a network without using messy Ethernet cables. Just like other adapters, it's plugged through USB port.

There are other accessories that may be used for working on this device. You can shop for accessories through shops and get a hold of the finest pieces that will build your project. It's even possible to find accessories with dual functionality.

Chapter 3
A Look at the Software

Just like other systems, utilizing Raspberry Pi 2 requires running a program for loading codes according to the function expected from the project. In this chapter, you'll learn about the program used for using Raspberry, focusing particularly on the following topics:

- Base framework

- Types of programs available

- Installation process

Raspbian Program

Raspberry Pi 2 is probably most known as the hardware, but the truth is it also comes with its own program to make the system work. Codes created and loaded using a different program may not work effectively in Raspberry Pi 2. Fortunately, Raspbian program is available for people who want to put their hands in building a system using RPi2.

Types of Program Available

There are different program types available that suit a programmer's needs or current setup available in their system. Software will work with the operating system and detects the type of board connected before placing the code. Types of programs available will suit people's needs are NOOBS and other third-party software.

New Out of the Box Software (NOOBS) is the Raspberry Pi developer's recommended program for beginners. It is contains an installer for operating system that loads Raspbian, the program used for programming Raspberry Pi 2 boards. This spftware is available for downloads at Raspberry Pi's website and can be installed in both MAC and Windows PC.

NOOBS is available in two versions. The regular NOOBS is an installer for both offline and network install features. It is updated regularly, so users will get the right option for their computers whenever they start to create their own Raspberry Pi 2 projects.

NOOBS Lite, on the other hand, is also an installer, but without Raspbian included in the system. Users need to install this component then download the other additional components later on. This option only let network install, but is also updated.

Aside from NOOBS and NOOBS Lite, there are other programs that offer Raspbian images from other third party developers. Expert developers created these programs that work with an array of operating systems. They are developed for Linux and Ubuntu operating systems. Many of them are also developed as open-source Raspbian, which advanced users can tweak themselves to create the perfect Raspbian software required by their project.

In downloading the program, the developers recommend NOOBS because of its easy to use features. However, advanced users will benefit from Ubuntu and Linux versions. They have the skills in managing these programs and tweak them through special configurations.

Obtaining NOOBS and Raspbian

There are several ways in obtaining the program version of Raspberry Pi 2. One is by downloading the program through the internet. The Foundation's website has a list of downloadable Raspbian programs and images that cater to developers needs. NOOB files are found on the top most part of the list being the most recommended choice among its main developers.

Users have two options in downloading these programs. First is by getting the compressed file from Raspberry Pi's website. When selected, users can directly download the file, extract and install as is.

Below the page are the Raspbian images developed by other developers, with most of them made for other operating systems like Ubuntu and Linux:

- Ubuntu Mate for Ubuntu desktop and available from ubuntu-mate.org

- Snappy Ubuntu Core for Snappy Ubuntu Core for Developers. Available at raspberrypi.org.

- Openelec for Open Embedded Linux Entertainment Centre. Available openelec.tv.

- OSMC Open Source Media Centre. Available at osmc.tv.

- Pidora for Fedora Remix. Available at pidora.ca.

- RISC OS. A non-linux distribution. Available at riscosopen.org.

Since they are developed by different developers, users will be directed to developers' website to download their programs. Links are available at the Foundation's website and will direct visitors to the actual page once clicked. Choose the right program for yo and see how it will work for you, your current resources, and project.

Installation Process

Installation process is important part of using Raspberry Pi 2. Users need to use the program for the programming process. Therefore, people need to know how to install this system.

A vital information to remember is the installation process may be different depending on the operating system used or the type of Raspbian program selected. Te general way of installing this program, however, includes the following procedures:

Choose the Installation Procedure Preferred

There are two ways to install Raspbian and NOOBs. One is by downloading the program from the website then use an SD card for he installation process. Te next option is getting the pre-installed SD card.

- **Get a Preinstalled SD card.** The preinstalled SD card is called as such with the availability of NOOBS itself into the device. It means that it's ready to install an dno need to go through the download process. NOOBS is already installed in the SD card and it will be ready to go. This SD card is available in recommended store, which are found in Raspberry Pi 2 website. No problem in getting this option because it's only cheap, costing around £4.

- **Download the Program.** Some people already have their own SD cards and will be used it for installing Raspbian. What users can do is download NOOBS or other Raspbian programs from third-party developer. Files are available in zip file. Users simply need to extract the downloaded file into the SD card.

Before downloading and extracting the program, experts recommend formatting the SD card first to ensure it will be free of files and ready to copy the Raspbian image. Several programs are available for formatting SD cards. Rapberry Pi recommends SD Formatter 4.0, which is available at SD Association's website. Choose the formatter compatible with your operating system and run. Follow the instructions written on the program and it should be ready to go. Plug in the SD card into your computer then remember the drive assigned to it. Launch SD formatter and format the SD card.

Once formatted, copy the extracted NOOBS file into the SD card. You can also extract files into the SD card as well directly if preferred. However, the former procedure is recommended if you wish to have a copy of Raspbian file to your computer, if you prefer to copy the files in another SD card in the future.

Boot Raspbrry Pi 2 Program

After formatting, plug all the computer peripherals and display cables into your system tower. Plug in the USB cable that is used with the PCB. The PCB should boot and will display a window listing available operating systems read for installation. Experts recommend choosing Raspbian for consistency with the PCB. Tick the box for Raspbian then click *Install*. Wait for the program to install, which may take several minutes.

Set Up the Raspberry Pi Data

Just like typical operating systems, Raspbian needs to be configured according to users' time zone and date. After installation, the newly installed Raspbian should display the Raspberry Pi configuration menu. Configure the time and date to make the operating system consistent with what you have.

Setup Raspberry Board for Users

Post-installation also lets users run different accessories that come with a board. A good example is a RPi2 camera. This menu also permits users create other users that will use the board. It serves as identifier for the device and lets individuals use the platform if necessary. Complete the setup by pressing tab and choose Finish.

Set Up the User Interface

Since Raspbian is like a typical operating system,users will need to login using their credentials before it can be used for programming. Login with the following credentials:

Username: pi

Password: raspberry

To set your expectation, be ready to not see the password as you type it. This is normal as a Linux security feature.

Type startx to Run the Graphic User Interface

Type "startx" as part of loading the graphic user interface. This should get your platform ready for programming.

After learning how to install the board and the software, you're ready to code your programs according to your project.

Chapter 4
Programming Basics

Programming is a crucial part in creating a project using Raspberry Pi 2. The commands placed create the expected function on a project. The system will interpret the code and let it connect to the mechanical part of PCB and deliver the desired function. In this section, you'll find out more about:

- The programming basics in Raspberry Pi 2

- What vital information is needed for coding

- Sample commands that will teach you create the program you need

Programming Basics

Every project done using a PCB requires programming. The program will be loaded into the device and it will execute it as an output. The programming basics include knowing the language typically used for Raspberry Pi 2.

The foundation recommends using Python as programming language for this product. If you are knowledgeable with Python for other programming purposes, you're in luck because you can use the same in Raspberry Pi 2.

However, the developer also stated that any programming language compiling for ARMv6 can be used with Raspberry Pi. Therefore other programming languages can be used like Java, Ruby, C, C++, and Scratch. If you plan to use these programming languages, you can find it installed on the Raspberry Pi, which means you can use your preferred coding program.

Now that you know about this programming, you must know the basic commands that will be identified by the system. Take note of the following details to get your system working.

Printing

Printing is the process of displaying a specific value set in the program. For example, you want to print or display "Raspberry is Awesome", code it as

print("Raspberry is Awesome")

Once entered, it will display the value to use as part of your code. This code is similar with commands in other projects that require code.

Variables

Variables refer to specific values needed for a specific code. Using a variable means declaring an alternative value that will be used throughout the program. The advantage of using a variable is programmers don't need to use all the values in the program. Using the raw value for programming can be confusing since a code can have several values. This can be mixed up and result to problems in coming up with the desired function.

To declare a variable, follow this code:

variable = value

In this code, the variable refers to any word serving like category related to a value. The value can be a number or a word that will be used in calculations or coding. Taking the code as an example, you can declare a variable as age and the number of the age that will be used in the code:

age = 20

name = "Jessie"

Word values used in a variable needs to be written with quotation marks. Numeric values don't need to be used with quotation marks since only a few codes include numbers.

This coding type will relate a single value to the variable. Nevertheless, coding also lets developers improve the coding and apply dynamic values with a declared variable. For instance, a variable's value can change as long as coded properly like the following:

variable = value

variable +=1

print(variable)

Take age for example with dynamic values:

age = 20

age += 2

print(age)

This code means that the value of the variable "age" will change in increments by 2. When the platform generated the code, it will print the code as required in *print(age)*.

Coding a command for your Raspberry Pi is going to depend on how you declare your variables. Remember to declare your variables properly to ensure the expected results will show using the dashboard. You can use this as the basis of your code in declaring variables and ensure they will show results.

Range

Range is important in declaring values. Range refers to the scale of numbers to be used for declaring an integer or a variable. This command is used in iteration where the command would need to list down certain values. A good example of declaring a range is the following code:

```
for i in range(value)

print(i)
```

Range will display the numbers that will be iterated. So, if you want to display the numbers within a specific range, you can type the following code:

```
for i in range(10)

print(i)
```

If you'll use this code, it will display the values equivalent in the declared value. So if it says 10, it means the numbers will be displayed are from 0 to 9, which is a total of 10 numbers. The number always begins with zero then continue up to the number called for in the code.

In some cases, you can also code to display the numbers within a specific number range. Placing the mere number of total numbers will always include zero in the range. if you don't want to include zero, place the beginning and end of the number range. code it like the following:

```
for i in range(1,10)

print(i)
```

In this code, you'll get the values starting from 1 instead of 0. It will also list down the numbers between the set range.

One of the common issues in setting range and iteration is not declaring the range value properly. For example:

```
for i in 5

print(i)
```

Since the code didn't set number 5 as a range for iteration, the platform won't read it as such and would just display the error message "TypeError: 'int' object is not iterable."

In this case, the number indicated is not declared as a range, and thus, it won't display a specific range of numbers.

Iteration

Iteration is the process of looping data types' values. This is a common practice for enumerating a list of numbers or letters to display in the platform. Take note of this code:

```
numbers = [4, 5, 6]

for number in numbers

    print(numbers)
```

In this code, "numbers" works as a datatype variable. Using iteration will list down the values declared in the code. When this code is processed, it will display the following values:

4

5

6

Naturally, you're not limited to using the word numbers used as a variable. Use whatever variable you wish to use. Be more descriptive in using the variable to help you know which item is which. Your code will have lots of words and it will be better if you can spot the variables easily.

The good thing about iteration is it won't only list down numbers. You can also assign a word value and it will list down the letters in it. Look at this code:

```
name = "Brownie"

for char in name

    print(name)
```

When you load this code it will list down the letters in the character with the first letter on top. It will print as:

B

r

o

w

n

i

e

If you'll analyze the code, using iteration still follows the same rules in declaring characters. It utilizes quotation marks for alphabets or characters while it doesn't use the punctuation for numbers. This is probably to indicate that a word is a declared value rather than a variable or a command.

Compare the iteration and range commands. In coding iteration, no need to declare a specific value into the code. Simply use the command and it will list down the value. However, values still need to be set in range because it was not declared during the first part of the code. Be mindful of the values to iterate to avoid getting an error message. And in case you meet an error message, carefully check the code you just placed and see for possible coding errors.

Lists

A list is also known as an array in other programming languages. Commands like iteration and range works together in coming up with lists of values. Brackets must be used with the numerical values to set the value to be listed. Each number to be listed must be separated with a

If Statements

Python programming also utilizes Boolean coding or commonly called as If statements. If statements let users control the flow of data coded in Raspberry Pi 2. Take a look at this if statement example:

name = "Jenny"

If len(name) > 5:

print("Lovely name,")

print(name)

else:

print("That's a nice name,")

print(name)

This code displays a conditional statement. A variable is declared on the first part of the code, which is the name. It then states that if the number of characters in a word is has more than 5 characters, it will print "Lovely name" then the name "Jenny". Otherwise, the code should print the values in the else statement. As long as declared properly, the code should be able to display the right results and use it for promoting a specific functions according to the declared condition.

If statements are often used in RPi 2 development where a developer wants to set conditions where the PCB and its components should function. A good example is when a LED should blink or when should it deactivate. Setting up an if statement can be quite confusing and tricky, but it should be simple as long as every value is declared accordingly.

Length

Length refers to the code that detects the number of characters or items in a list. Code it by using the term "len". Example:

```
name = "Jane"

print(len(name)) #4

girls = ["Jamie", "Jane", "Jenny", "Jesse"]

print(len(girls)) #4
```

In this example, the variable name is declared with a value, "Jane". As a value, the code is going to detect the number of characters in the declared value. It's different, however, when it comes to declaring the length of values declared as a list. Instead of detecting the number of characters, the code will detect the number of items within the range. Brackets are used as indicator that the items listed are included in a range and that it should be counted as is.

Indentation

Several coding elements like symbols are important like brackets, semicolons and parenthesis. For Python programming, indentation is among the crucial coding elements in terms of bringing several codes together.

Numerous programming languages utilize curly braces in wrapping lines of codes within a program. Wrapping them together means all the lines are included in a specific code. Being included means it should have an effect on how the values should be represented in a code. All indented items are considered as a part of a function, which means they should display according to the what the code requires. Look at this example:

```
for i in range(3):

print("A")

print("B")

print("C")
```

Once processed, it will display as:

A

B

C

A

B

C

A

B

C

Looking at it closely, the range indicates three instances of the values to be printed. Since all commands for the letters are indented, it means they must be looped three times as indicated on the range command.

See this code with some unindented parts:

for i in range(3):

  print("A")

print("B")

print("C")

Its value will display as

  A

  A

  A

  B

  C

Only the indented part of the function is the online that that has been looped as indicated in the range cod. The remaining codes simply printed as is. This is because the platform didn't identify the last two codes as part of the function for i in *range(3)* due to the lack of indentation. Therefore, they are interpreted as a different function and printed without following the same iteration function.

Comments

commenting is important in programming. It serves as vital notes in coding a specific line or command. First time Raspberry Pi 2 and program users need to use notes to remind them of the expected code function. To denote a function, use multiple quotation marks. For example:

for i in range(3): """This is a comment

  print("A")

""""This is a multiline comment

enclosed by quotation marks

""""

Multiple quotation marks must be used because using a single pair of quotation marks will only make the comment look like a typical character value and will be interpreted as a part of the code. The problem is your comment has more words and characters than what the coding platform expected.

Chapter 5
Important things to Remember

Using RPi 2 and its paired program can be simple, but several points must be remembered in using both platforms. Take note of the following tips and reminders that you'll find helpful as you continue with the project:

Protect Your Mini Computer

one of the great things about RPI2 is it is a compact mini computer. You'll get it as is and bare without accessories unless you get them together with the package.

But even if you get it as is, you may still want to get it protected by using a case. This board is considered as your investment, which means you don't want it to get damaged you continue with the project. As a beginner, there's no guarantee that you'll complete the project quickly. You may want to protect it from damages caused by shock. A case is readily available in different online stores and an be purchased as an add-on. The case may even come with other components that can be helpful for your project.

Common accessories that come with Raspberry Pi 2 is a case with built-in heatsink and thermal pads, just like in regular computers. They will keep the machine from overheating, especially if you plan to use it for computing projects. Aside from cooling, it is a hard case that will protect all the parts installed on the board. They are thick enough serving as chassis for extra protection.

Always Update Firmwares

Since raspberry pi 2 can be used for computing, firmware update emerges as an important procedure to ensure the project will work. In typical computers, updating firmware is a solution whenever a component failed to work properly. Getting a firmware update will also help in ensuring your project will run smoothly.

After installing the program and setting the board, set firmware updates for the board and for the program, then wait for the board to reboot. After rebooting, get additional components that you'll need for your project. Commonly downloaded programs are VLC (for media), Chromium (web browser), and LibreOffice (a document processing platform).

Get a WiFi Adapter

some projects require WiFi connectivity and is required to get them together with the board. However, having a wifi adapter is also important for future use. Get it with the product itself and test out how it should be used.

Avoid Taking Photos with Raspberry Pi 2

Although camera attachment and interface are available, people who have tried this device doesn't recommend taking photos, especially using Xenon flash. Reports claimed that taking photos cause the board to shut down or reset.

This problem is caused by the U16 chip installed in the newest Raspberry Pi 2. The chip is said to be light-sensitive and shuts down whenever it detects flash from Xenon flashes due to photoelectric reaction. Experience developers reported that covering this chip using components similar to BluTack can protect it from resetting.

In case you can to use other cameras with flashes, you can work without problems with LED flashes, like those found in smartphones and tablets.

Although solutions for protecting the U16 chip is available like covering with a BluTack material, it is still advisable not to take photo with Xenon flashes. Not simply because it resets the system, which means you need to reboot the board and load incomplete codes, but to combat restarting's negative effects on your system. For instance, a system abruptly resetting can damage your SD card used for storage or running the operating system. This means that all your hard work by setting up the codes and the operating system environment will be lost due to resetting.

Although many people expect that this problem will be solved in future Raspberry releases, the foundation hasn't released any news about fixing this problem.

Say Goodbye to Retrogaming

Raspberry became famous among hobbyists and developers due to its ability to support retrogaming. This feature lets developers load and run their gaming ROMs through RPi's emulation support. However, this feature is currently not supported on the new device. The reason is processor compatibility.

RetroPie, a solution used by retro gaming systems, requires enhancements to be compatible with RPi 2's quadcore processor. Now that this is not supported, those who want to use this PCB for improving PSX and N64 game emulation.

Don't Look for Power on/off Button

As a computing unit, people often look for a power button on these devices. Naturally, users want to make sure that they are activating and deactivating the PCB properly. Some PCBs have their own power buttons, but not RPi 2.

To activate the device, users simply need to plug it in through its power supply and it should activate. Turning off, however, requires a bit of effort. Turn it off by using the device's graphical environment. Exit to open the terminal then key in the command "*sudo halt -h*", excluding the quotation marks. Keying this command will trigger the LED light to turn off, indicating that power stopped circulating within the system circuitry. Wait several seconds again after the LED turned off to ensure that the SD card has stopped operating. Don't pull the PCB system out right away because it might still be using the operating system image. It may render the SD card useless, even to a point where you can't install anything in it anymore.

Start Trying Your Board with a Few Project Examples

Now that you know the basics of using and installing Raspberry Pi 2, you can start getting into your own projects by trying out these cool recommendations for beginners.

- Internet Radio
- Raspberry Smartphone
- Raspberry Social Media Platform and Media Player
- Color Your Workstation Using LEDs
- Content Handler
- Extremely Lovely LED Lamp

Conclusion
Do not fill out I will fill out Conclusion myself

Thank you again for downloading this book!

I hope this book was able to help you to create amazing projects with Raspberry Pi 2.

The next step is to try out these projects and continue mastering the skills needed in developing high-end RPi 2 projects.

Finally, if you enjoyed this book, then I'd like to ask you for a favor, would you be kind enough to leave a review for this book on Amazon? It'd be greatly appreciated!

Click here to leave a review for this book on Amazon!

Thank you and good luck!

Your Free Bonus

Arduino For Beginners

How to get started with your arduino, including Arduino basics, Arduino tips and tricks, Arduino projects and more!

Introduction

I want to thank you and congratulate you for downloading the book, *"Arduino For Beginners - How to get started with your arduino, including Arduino basics, Arduino tips and tricks, Arduino projects and more!"*.

This book contains proven steps and strategies on how to use Arduino in your tech projects.

Arduino became a popular solution that extends computing and robotics to individuals outside technology field. Hobbyists can do these projects at home while gaining all the advantages this product offers.

This book will teach you all about Arduino and the working components behind its functions. As a beginner, this book teaches you of the concepts, important Arduino parts, basic coding fundamentals and many more.

Towards the end of the book, you'll find several tips and tricks, as well as beginner-level project ideas that will help you master Arduino!

Thanks again for downloading this book. I hope you enjoy it!

Table of Contents

Introduction...27

Chapter 1. Arduino Basics: Knowing Arduino..................................30

Chapter 2. Arduino Basics: Arduino Models....................................34

Chapter 3. Arduino Basics: A Look at the Hardware.........................37

Chapter 4. Arduino Basics: A Look at the Software...........................45

Chapter 5. Troubleshooting and Fixing Arduino Issues.....................53

Chapter 6. Additional Tips and Tricks...56

Conclusion..59

Chapter 1. Arduino Basics: Knowing Arduino

The amazing world computing kept on stirring the minds of individuals interested in this field. They want to get their hands into technological projects using a simple circuit board and program codes. Arduino makes it possible for people outside technology field to create their own devices with specific functions.

In this section, you'll learn about:

- Arduino and its definition

- Where it's used

- Available Arduino types

- Arduino's limitations

Definition

Arduino is a microcontroller developed as an open-source system. It's powered by a chip and composed of different components soldered on the board. It resembles a mini motherboard used in an array of projects.

Arduino is also programmable according to the required functions in a project. Programs will be used to assign certain pins to execute specific tasks. Parts and pins are identified using the labels printed on the board. You'll more about parts and in Chapter 3.

The term "Arduino" is often referred to the actual mini board. However, Arduino board needs to use its software version, also known as Arduino software. It's used for programming commands that indicate the board's purpose or function. More details about Arduino program will be discussed on Chapter 3.

The Advantage of Using Arduino

Many people appreciated this product as it's designed to make robotics and mini computing accessible to regular users. Arduino is marketed for prototyping hobbyists, novice engineers, and those who want to try simple robotics despite the lack of engineering expertise. Everyone who wants to explore robotics and computing can now do projects right at their homes.

Another advantage is its inexpensive price. An Andruino board's price starts at $20 and up depending on the number of installed parts, part types, and slots. The price alone is suitable for beginners who are technically testing Arduino-powered robotics and computing. Hobbyists can complete small projects, which don't usually cost a lot of money, but still offers the features required by developers.

Arduino's open-source and programmable platform brings another benefit. Being an open-source system, Arduino can perform functions required by developers by uploading source codes to get their projects going.

Long-term advantage is using Arduino can help hobbyists build their own boards. Users learn Arduino's architecture by using the board and their functions. Developers can then personalize their future boards according to their projects' complex system.

Finally, Arduino works with different components, allowing designers to be more playful with their project ideas. Projects can be as simple as activating blinking LEDs or blinking or projects that are more mechanical in nature.

What Projects can You Do with Ardruino?

Arduino is a complete device that lets developers do virtually any project. Common and simple projects include developing a small computer for cars, social media "like" counters, MIDI controllers, and a lot more. People who are more ambitious can build small robots, given that the right board is used. Depending on the design and functionalities, a mini robot project may require complicated development.

This board is capable of supporting all these projects through its components, which you'll learn in Chapter 3.

Limitations

Although this system allows hobbyists to do almost everything, Arduino still has its limitations. Its inability to capture and record videos is its main downside. The board's specs are insufficient to support these tasks, which is very different from typical computers and portable devices. These devices are meant for media recording and designed with appropriate components.

However, Arduino is capable of projecting images or graphics through an external display. Unlike capturing videos, projecting won't use as much resources and storage from the board. Also, utilizing an exterior display will handle data conversion to display images or other information. Developers must create a special configuration to make this setup possible.

Available Types

Arduino comes in different models and types. Each model possesses unique features and matches a specific function. As of now, Arduino is distributed in three models. Certain models are available in several variants that cater to special projects' requirements.

Important Things to Remember

Several reminders in using Arduino in your project:

Get the Right Arduino According to Project Requirements

Arduino has different pin numbers and parts depending on the model. Getting the wrong model will result to system incompatibility. Some pins may not work properly when used in other boards.

Another issue is using the wrong board can be confusing for the developer. Project guides specify pin numbers and parts. Being a novice Arduino user, you might get confused when you don't find jumpers, pin numbers, and other vital parts for the project.

Avoid incompatibility issues by reading the guide well. Verify the required board before shopping. Some guides give a link to the indicated Arduino model, which you can click and purchase the recommended board.

Arduino Development is Not Limited to Hardware Knowledge

Using Arduino for a project is not limited to understanding its parts and their respective functions. Your project's success also depends if the code is properly written and successfully loaded to the system. Arduino requires learning the coding process and its fundamental concepts. You must also know how to operate the software and designing codes.

This book will discuss more about coding in Chapter 4.

Chapter 2. Arduino Basics: Arduino Models

Two Arduino models are ideal for beginners' use: Arduino Uno and Arduino Mega. Their features and specifications will be discussed in this section. Other board types will also be mentioned without detailed information since they are meant for advanced Arduino users.

Android Uno

Arduino Uno is the most recommended board for beginners. It's designed for small projects. Similar Uno versions with the same features can be used if preferred.

Uno runs on ATMega328 chip and uses USB, AC/DC adapter or battery as power source. This all-purpose board supports up to 12V power using a wall-wart adapter. Avoid using higher current than 12 volts to avoid risk of overheating. For projects requiring lower current, it has a 5V pin that supports 5 volts of power and other lower voltages. Typical batteries can be utilized as power source, but be wary of the power source draining faster with frequent use.

This model's features include 14 digital input/output (I/O) pins and six analog input pins. Six of the digital I/O pins can be used as PWM. The analog pins' resolution is the maximum of 10 bits , delivering 1024 different reading values.

Model specs include 8-bit CPU, 2KB SRAM, 32 KB flash memory, 1 KB EEPROM, 16MHz clock speed. Its form factor is 2.1 inches by 2.7 inches rectangular board.

Uno's main advantage is having simple circuitry that utilizes small footprint, making it the perfect Arduino for smaller projects. Other pros are accessibility. Uno is widely available and affordable at $30. Users can also find many Uno accessories and shields.

A lot of those who used this board share their projects online. Novice Arduino users have more project options to try with these guides. Guides shared include making a talking clock, thermostat, simple blinking LEDs and many more.

Someone embarking in an Arduino project will find the right projects to begin with through the massive online references available.

As for the disadvantages, this product can run out of pins, particularly if the user won't utilize an external integrated circuit. Another downside is the absence of high memory, which keeps people from using it for special projects.

Arduino Mega 2560

Arduino Mega 2560 is the next recommended Arduino for beginners' projects. It's used for bigger projects that require higher specs. Individuals who are experienced in using this device end up making complicated projects that are guaranteed to work with Mega. Beginners can also try using this device if they aim for complex projects that their current skills can accomplish.

Mega is almost the same as Uno, except that it has more features, especially I/O pins. It has 70 I/O pins that let users plug more components. Out of 70 pins, 54 of them are digital I/O pins and the remaining are analog pins. Specs include 8KB SRAM, 256KB flash memory, and 4KB EEPROM. Due to its massive features, this Arduino can hold programs four times larger than Uno's supported capacity.

Using this device has a lot of advantages. Aside from massive number of I/O pins, it also comes in two variations that meet developers' requirements further. The first variation is *Due* that has 32-bit ARM, which is faster and offers more resources to support advanced projects. Nevertheless, it only runs at 3.3V power.

Another variation is ADK, which is designed for Android phones. This is a common choice for individuals wanting to explore mobile device computing.

Other advantages are the generous memory capacity and storage space for coding and running programs. It can run massive projects without using external integrated circuits and as long as projects carefully thought out. Just like with Uno, individuals using Mega will find a lot of projects online provided by individuals who have been using the device for a long time.

Although its features are regarded ideal for a lot of beginners dreaming of larger projects, it also has its disadvantages like the need for modifying codes. Guides shared for this Arduino often requires people to change codes slightly depending on the pin numbers. Another disadvantage is it's more expensive than Arduino Uno, which may not be as practical for beginners. Although it's only twice as much in terms of price, it may not be recommended due to chances of damaging the board while in the middle of setting up the project.

Its availability in stores as well as accessories needed to execute the project with it may also be challenging. It's not as widely available as Uno. Users may need to look for Mega in in overseas stores. As for accessories, it doesn't have as many shields available in stores. You'll find out more about shields in the next section.

Other Arduino Models

Other Arduino models are available for higher end projects. These models won't be discussed in detail since they are not recommended for beginners.

- *Arduino Pro.* Arduino Pro is for more advanced and professional developers. It has similarities with Uno in terms of power capacity and the lack of header pins. Connections must be soldered onto the board for them to function. Hence, using Pro requires expert or professional handling. It's also ideal for projects that must be permanently embedded together. Pro variations include Mini, Fio and Micro.

- *LilyPad.* LilyPad differs from all discussed Arduino types due to shape. Instead of having rectangular form factors, this device comes in round shape with flower-like pattern. This device is ideal for constructing wearable systems and e-textiles. It's washable and those who have used it claimed that using a mild soap shouldn't be a problem in washing the device.

Chapter 3. Arduino Basics: A Look at the Hardware

The main board is serves as the core of an Arduino's project. Its parts convert data to execute require functions. This chapter teaches you about:

- Arduino parts and their respective labels.

- Tools used for setting up the project.

- Basic procedures beginners must know.

Parts

Arduino is comparable to a regular computer motherboard with its parts working together in distributing signals from input to output channels, power distribution, and execute coded functions. Parts placements or their locations within the board are different depending on the models. As a beginner, you must learn some basic parts that are crucial for your project.

Processor or Integrated Circuit

Just like computers, a processor serves as the center of entire board operation. Due to the Arduino's small form factor, its processor also comes small in size with varying capacities depending on the board model.

An Integrated Circuit (IC) can be long or square black plate with metal legs often placed above the Analog pins and Power pins section. It acts as Arduino's main processing unit or brain. Different IC types are compatible for specific project, which stresses the importance of verifying required Arduino before purchasing.

Power Supply

A power supply is the electricity gateway used for activating the entire board. The electricity will flow through embedded circuits towards the connected parts. Power transmitted will activate the parts to do their tasks like receiving and analyzing signals then process conversion. To ensure proper board function, it should have smooth power flow that keeps the system activated.

Power supply sources can be placed through USB port or a barrel jack. USB connection, just like in flash drives, distributes electricity throughout the board. The USB port's size in Arduino is the same as those installed in computers. The size is enough to fit a typical USB cable. However, not all boards have USB ports, which can be a problem if you prefer using USB connection as power gateway. Check the power supply source first online before purchasing an Arduino board.

USB port's function is not limited to power distribution. It's also used for loading codes to the board. You'll write the code on your computer then load it to the board through USB just like the usual file transfer process.

Another power supply source is the barrel jack or power jack. A power jack is a typical external power source. It got its name due to its barrel-like shape embedded on an exposed board. It looks like a typical power jack for mobile devices and works with an adapter. The barrel jack is installed on a board using three metal prongs that conduct electricity.

Power Supply Jumpers

Power supply jumpers let you toggle or choose between two power supplies. Activate your preferred power source using the jumper and it will temporarily deactivate other power source. For example, your board can get power through USB connection and an adapter through the power jack. But for now, you prefer getting power through USB connection. Set the jumper to USB and the board will only receive power from USB connection. Therefore, the system won't power up upon plugging an adapter into the jack. If you prefer otherwise, set the jumper to power jack and the system will activate once an adapter is used.

The power jumper looks like a switch placed in between labels "USB and EXT". It's located in between the USB port and the power jack or power regulator.

Keep in mind that a jumper is not always labeled. The board's diagram makes it easy for advanced Arduino users to spot the jumper. Several board models may not have this option. Verify this information by visiting the board's website or downloading its data sheet.

Analog Pins

Analog pins are used for transferring data or signals from an analog sensor. You'll locate a group of analog pins by looking for the label "Analog In," which stands for "Analog Input". The analog signal or data will then be converted to digital data shown on displays like LCD displays or external graphics output. An Arduino can have more than one pin depending on the model. The set of analog pins are often located at the lower right corner, if you're looking at the board with the power jack on the lower left side.

Digital Pins

Located at the topmost side of the board are the digital pins, which are used for input/output devices. It can be used for reading digital signals or data then interpreting it to digital output. A common example is digital input from pushing a button which then translates to output like lighting a LED bulb. Just like analog input, a board can have several digital pins based on the model.

Reset Button

Reset Button functions similarly as gaming consoles' reset buttons. When pushed, it will ground and restart Arduino's code. This component is helpful for people using non-repetitive codes. It looks like a typical button with "Reset" label. The button's placement varies on the Arduino model.

Power Pins

The power pins refer to the pins connected for power distribution. It is a group of pins working for this function. This group is often found beside the analog pins group and labeled "Power". Pins under this group are:

- **Ground** (GRN). Ground serves as a reference point in connecting components with varying voltage capacities. It sets a common ground that prevents high voltage current from flowing thru low voltage connections. Ground connections let you install a 12V part to a 5V Arduino. The number of ground connections varies on model. Ground pins are often found with analog and digital pin groups.

- **Pulse-Width Modulation (PWM)**. Pulse-width modulation is another term referring to a digital signal type. It allows Arduino to carry out sophisticated circuitry control like fading LED light through analog output simulation.

- **Analog Reference (AREF)**. Users may or may not use this pin depending on the project. Oftentimes, it sets analog input pins' upper limits, usually from zero to 5V.

- **IOREF**. This pin indicates the required voltage to operate the microcontroller. IOREF values are different across Arduino models. For example, Arduino UNO supplies 5V to IOREF pin while Duo supplies 3V.

LED indicator

An Arduino has one LED light serving as power indicator. It lights up when the board is connected to a power source. An activated LED means power is distributed properly throughout the board. Failing to light up indicates probable circuitry issues that affect power distribution or power source problems.

Voltage Regulator

The voltage regulator is a component that stabilizes power's voltage as it flows within the board. However, it can't tolerate extremely high voltage power sources. Experts recommend not to plug Arduinos to a power source with over 20 volts.

This component is located the barrel jack and USB port and characterized by a rectangular black panel with three protruding legs.

Components

An Arduino board is only a single part of a project. Other components will be installed together with it to ensure the project will function as expected. Aside from Arduino PCB, the following components must be verified on guides and purchased for the project:

Shields

Shields are components placed on top of the main Arduino board to extend its capabilities. These components can be purchased together with Arduino PCB at the same shop. Although it may look like a cover for Arduino, it has similar design with the main PCB, which makes it work like a feature extender.

Different types of shields are available that will work well depending on the project. Examples of commonly used shields are the following:

- **Xbee.** Xbee is a shield that serves as wireless communication gateway in between Arduino boards up to 100 feet in distance when indoors. The distance capacity can increase by up to 300 feet when used in an outdoor space. It needs the Maxtream Xbee Zibgee module as the main component to function as a wireless connection device.

- **Motor Control.** This module lets users control and manipulates DC motors and reading their encoders.

- **Custom Shields.** Some developers think that customizing their own shields is the best solution for their projects. They want to customize the function they'll get in using the additional device. Luckily, developers can create their own shields by following guides online. Beginners are recommended to use specific guides for custom shields. Be reminded, however, that customizing another PCB may require expertise depending on the series complexity.

Wire

Wires are the actual connectors that aid electricity flow or data transfer. They are the basic components used in developing technical systems. Developers may refer to any component or device that conducts electricity in between other Arduino devices as wire. There are two types of wire used with Arduino: the physical wire and wire gauges.

The physical wire comes in solid or stranded wire categories. These wire categories depend on the wire flexibility called for by a project. A solid wire is ideal for a project that doesn't need it to bend or flex. Placing at least one solid wire can simplify the work required for Arduino projects. A good example of such project is in buildings - the wire won't bend and the system will only use a single connection instead of several stranded wires, which have the tendency to bend excessively and result to problematic handling.

Stranded wire is the most flexible wire often used as appliances cords or cables for audio and video output.

Wire gauges are utilized with breadboards. It supports the installation of 22 gauge wires, but it can also handle a gauge or two if needed. It can have headers like female headers, which can't be used for wire insertion, but will work effectively in prototyping projects. Many novice developers may have a hard time choosing between 20 and 22 wire gauges. The 20-gauge wire may be slightly dependable than 22 gauge ones, but will certainly work.

Breadboard

Breadboard refers to the component utilized for circuit construction and testing. It looks like a small white board with many square holes in it. A breadboard is usually incorporated in a prototyping project. There are different types of breadboard that meet specific project demands. A common type is a solderless breadboard. Wires are inserted through the breadboard holes then connect on the metal strips below. Utilizing a breadboard keeps users from soldering wires and connectors and still retains them in place.

Capacitor

This small component retains and releases electrical charge in a circuit connection. It usually has two charging plates and an additional material that controls electricity discharge. They come in different types, but indicated on Arduino's product descriptions for buyers' reference.

They can be produced with different features, with some sold mainly for storage due to their sizes. Store charge capacity is represented in Farads (F).

Resistor

A resistor resists electricity flow, which guarantees smooth electricity flow within the system. It's a must-have component on PCBs for protection in instances of power fluctuation, which affects the entire project. Their capacities are measured in Ohms (R) or (Ω).

Inductor

An inductor is a solution that keeps electrical energy within a magnetic field. It's a wire coil that produces a magnetic field whenever current is distributed throughout the board. Energy increase during distribution promotes higher energy stored in the field. When it decreased, energy is converted and released as electrical power. Induction capacity is measured in Henrys (H).

Diode

A diode is a device that permits one-way or unidirectional electricity flow. Several types of diode types are available with specific functions. The most common is light emitting diode (LED) and photo diode that detects light.

LED

As a diode, LED can produce a specific wavelength of light upon receiving specific electricity voltage or also called the forward voltage. As an example, a bright LED means it receives high voltage electricity and dimmer when lower voltage circulates in the PCB.

Since this device doesn't have any limiting feature, it receives the full voltage and causes overheating. Overheating causes LED to be burned out easily. A burned out LED will still activate with decreased brightness unlike its original wavelength.

Pushbutton

A pushbutton is a device that controls electricity flow in a circuit. It can either complete or stop electricity flow with a trigger on the button. There are many types of pushbuttons compatible with specific projects and come with special configurations. A favorite among developers is the momentary switch.

Transistor

A transistor is a device that permits current flow between two points by utilizing a third component. Current flow happens if the third point of contact is present or not. It comes with three leads and available in two types.

Relay

Relay depends on mechanical movement to complete a connection between two points. It comes with a special type of contact switch utilizing solenoid as one of its components. It can switch mechanisms to interchange low DC current with larger AC currents.

Included Procedures

Several procedures are required to bring a board together. Circuits must be connected by plugging wires and setting a ground to produce a good point of reference for electrical current.

Perhaps the most challenging part of using this board is soldering. Soldering is the process of connecting two conductors together by melting a lead on the connection then letting it cool down. Once cooled, the lead becomes hard enough to keep the wires together in place.

Chapter 4. Arduino Basics: A Look at the Software

Studying Arduino software is the next lesson to study after learning the hardware. Learning about the software is as important as complex coding is needed to generate desired results in building a project. Guides can help you get familiarized with the software.

In this section, you'll learn about:

- Arduino software in general.

- Software installation procedures.

- Connecting the hardware with the software.

- Loading Codes to Arduino.

- Coding fundamentals.

Getting to Know Arduino Software

Arduino software is the program used for coding and transferring codes to the hardware. Different types of Arduino software are available and compatible with major operating systems. The latest version is Arduino 1.6.4., an opensource program with easy to use interface once installed, with versions compatible with Windows, Mac and Linux. Although installation procedures across operating system types are different, users must follow a standard rule in uploading the programmed code.

The Installation Process

The general rule is installing the Arduino software first before using the Arduino PCB. Installation procedures are as follows:

1. Look and select Arduino board from online shops. Aside from the board, you must also get a USB cable to connect the board to the computer. Different Arduino models come with their compatible USB cables. Be mindful of the cable required by reading the model's description.

2. Download the program compatible with your computer's operating system. The program is available at Arduino's website, with the standard Arduino software listed first being the most recommended platform to use. Other program options are available, but they may require special installation procedures. Furthermore, using another program tends to void your Arduino's warranty. Verify these procedures first and see the instance when your product's warranty may be voided.

3. Extract and install the downloaded program.

4. Plug the board to the computer using the USB cable after installation. Some Arduinos like Uno and Mega obtain power through USB connection. These boards should power up immediately once plugged to a computer.

   Some models supporting external and USB power sources should be configured properly to receive electricity through USB cable. A good example is Diecimila, which supports two types of electricity sources. Set the jumper, the switch-like device discussed in the previous chapter, to USB for now as its power source. Once configured, plug the board to the computer. Its LED will light up once electricity flows throughout the circuitry.

5. Install Arduino drivers. Just like external devices, your computer's operating system must install Arduino's driver first before it can receive codes. The board works like a plug and play device. The operating system will detect the new device once plugged in and install its drivers. However, this procedure may fail since you need to configure the driver manually.

   Once drivers failed to install, open Device Manager and look at Ports (COM & LPT). Your Arduino should be listed under this group as "Arduino (Model) (COMxx)". If not listed, search under "Other Devices" and look for "Unknown Device". It means your computer detected the newly plugged device, but it can't identify the new component correctly due to the lack of pre-installed drivers. Right click or double click on the Arduino model and look for "Update Driver Software" option. You'll be directed to another dialog box. Choose "Browse my computer for driver software". Locate the Arduino installer and look for the "Drivers" folder that comes with it. Select "Arduino.inf" to install.

There instances, however, when "Arduino.inf" is missing. Using older IDE versions like 1.0.3. and other earlier versions often cause this issue. In this scenario, look for the driver that has the Arduino's model name in it. For instance, if you're using Arduino Uno, look for the file "Arduino UNO.inf". Selecting the file will cause the operating system to install the file and it's ready to go.

Differences in operating system may also affect the software installation process. Installation is an instant process in newer operating systems like Windows 7 or Vista. Installation in Windows XP can be slightly complicated with its older interface developed earlier by Microsoft.

When the device is plugged in, it should display the "Add New Hardware" dialog box that installs the Arduino software. Don't let the operating system look for drivers in Windows Update. Choose "Install from a list or specified location (Advanced)". Click next and you'll be directed to the next prompts. Tick the box for "Search for the best driver in these locations" and uncheck "Search removable media". Tick "Include this location in the search" and look for the drivers/FTDI USB Drivers directory.

Since it's possible that available drivers are outdated, download newer driver versions by visiting FTDI website. Click next and the system should start searching for the new device. It will report about finding a "USB Serial Converter". Click it and complete the installation process. Once done, the newly installed hardware should be found under Ports (COM & LPT).

6. Open Arduino software to see sample codes. It comes with pre-set codes that can be used as reference for beginners. Load the blink example in the program by clicking File > Examples > Basics > Blink. You will see a list of code together with the description or function of what the code should do on the product. For example, the code indicates that this command will turn a LED on and off with a duration of a second each run repeatedly.

7. Load example codes to Arduino. Select the board type under Tools > Board. Clicking on the Arduino model will place a check on the selected option. Next, choose the port allotted for the device. Usually, the Arduino board ports are COM3 or higher. The first two ports, COM1 and COM2, are usually designated for hardware serial ports. If you're unsure of the right port, open the menu first the look for the available ports. List them down if needed. Disconnect your board then re-open the menu. The missing port should be the one assigned for your Arduino. Reconnect it and select to upload the code.

After selecting the port, click Upload to load the programmed code. You'll know that codes are being processed and uploaded light flashes on the board. The computer will display a dialog box saying "Done uploading," which means the code has been successfully uploaded.

8. Observe the effects. Wait for several seconds after completing the upload and you'll see the board's LED lights blinking.

Coding Fundamentals

Although you're a beginner, you must know more about coding fundamentals or the basic terms you will often see in writing codes. Being knowledgeable of the terms will help you code faster in the long run.

Variables

Variables refer to the container used for keeping the data. It declares a data's value, indicates its name, and highlights the function type expected. The code syntax is:

Type Variable = Value

So, if you have pin number 14 and int as a type, you can code it as:

int pin = 14

This value will be applied throughout the new codes placed in the Arduino program. Typing the value frequently is unnecessary. The system will automatically detect the value and function according to the set variable. For example, in this code:

pinMode(pin, OUTPUT)

Since you've declared the value of pin in "int pin=14" code as 14, the system will use the same pin value all throughout the code.

The coding process will make you think if declaring value through variable is necessary. Why not just type the value over and over again than write complex and confusing code? The main advantage is you will only declare the value once and it will be used repeatedly in the code. No need to type the value manually because the software will automatically detect it.

Declaring a variable's value can be done right at the beginning of the code to declare the global value. When you declare a global value, the software should use the assigned value throughout the code. For example,

int pin = 14

void setup()

{

pinMode(pin, OUTPUT);

}

void loop()

{

digitalWrite(pin, High)

}

This code has two functions, which you'll learn more in the next section. Notice that the pin value assignment is placed at the top, which means the value will be global or used throughout the entire code.

Changing the pin's value is also possible with a simple command. Nevertheless, you must be careful in declaring the value because they may or may not change the value then result to an error message. An example of coding to change the value is this code:

int pin = 14

```
void setup()

{

 pin = 15

 pinMode(pin, OUTPUT);

}

void loop()

{

 digitalWrite(pin, High)

}
```

The value of pin in digitalWrite() part will also change as it's assigned on top of the code as a global value.

If you want to change a pin's value in a certain function, you can type it in a manner where the value is only interpreted as a part of a specific function. For example:

```
void setup()

{

 int pin = 15;

 pinMode(pin, OUTPUT);

 digitalWrite(pin, High);

}
```

In this case, the new value of 15, will only be used in this function.

There are instances when you may experience error message after declaring a value. Example:

```
void setup()

{
```

```
int pin = 15;

pinMode(pin, OUTPUT);

digitalWrite(pin, High);

}
void loop()

{

digitalWrite(pin, LOW);

}
```

You've declared the pin value, but the value for *digitalWrite* under *loop()* won't read and use 15. Reason being is the pin value assigned is not within the function's scope. Assigned value is for *setup()*, but not for *loop()*. Regardless of where the code is placed, the system won't be able to recognize the code you just placed.

Function

A function refers to the line of code used to define a task. When loaded, a function will execute the task as described in the code. Programmers can even use a single function and use it several times if desired.

Since a function serves an indicator, new Arduino users would ask if placing the code in function segments is still necessary. Placing a full code in segmented functions has its benefits, with organization as the main reason. It helps developers organize their codes. Functions' keywords indicate developers about what they can do once loaded to a board.

Another advantage of segmentation is it aids developers to spot their needed codes immediately. Arduino developers must use some functions multiple times. Referring to the previously used codes will be less demanding than typing them again, saving developers more time in creating their programs.

Dissecting a Function

In Arduino, a function needs to have a *setup()* and *loop()*. They are the main function codes that beginner must learn. On the other hand, the system will know that the new code is outside through brackets, which are required coding symbols.

Look at the following code to dissect the parts of a function:

int myMultiplyFunction(int x, int y) {

int result;

result = x * y

return result;

}

- **Function name.** A function name refers to the task to be done in the code. In creating a simple calculation code, it will be the variable to be displayed or what the function is for. For instance, the function name in the aforementioned code is *myMultiplyFunction*

- **Parameters.** Parameters refer to the value a function inherited. In this case, the parameters are *int x* and *int y*.

- **Return Statement.** A return statement refers to the type of data that matches the declaration. Return statement is easy to spot in this code because it has the word "return".

- **Datatype of returned data.** This is the returned value after the code has been activated. When a value returned, it will show *int*, which is found in the first part of the code. In case there's no value was returned after loading a code, then the datatype will be *void*.

Now that you know what these codes stand for, you will learn about sample projects that you can do on your own. For now, coding won't discussed in depth with you being a beginner Coding won't be describe in detail at this point with you being a beginner. However, you'll see more codes upon doing some projects.

Chapter 5. Troubleshooting and Fixing Arduino Issues

There are instances when your Arduino program or hardware won't function properly. The problem can be caused by software or hardware issues like incompatibility. This section is dedicated to troubleshooting and solving Arduino problems on software and hardware level.

Can't Load Programs on Arduino

Loading program should be easy given that you have the right program and the right board. There are several reasons why you can't load codes into the system. The problem can range from missing the right drivers, board, or using the wrong port in the software. In terms of hardware problems, the problem can be caused by problematic physical connection or the device firmware.

Solution: Verify Board Model and Configured Model

The first solution is double-checking the Arduino model configured on the program. Some users tend to select the wrong type of board on the program. Verify the model used then access Tools > Board menu on Arduino software. Once you have selected the right board type, you can reload the code and see if it will be loaded.

Another thing to check is the type of microcontroller on the board. For example, several Arduino boards have ATmega 160 microcontroller, particularly the older boards. The newer ones have ATmega328. If you're confused as to what to choose, you can look at the microcontroller on the board and select it on the device.

Driver problem is also a common problem why the system won't load the code. See if the driver is installed by checking Tools > Serial Port. Be sure that the board is connected to the computer in verifying this information.

Another place to check is the device manager in your computer. Look if there are some items that are marked yellow or unidentified in the device. If you don't know some drivers that probably causing the problem, the marked driver should be the one belonging to Arduino board. You may need to reinstall or update the driver by accessing its properties and installing the driver. You can review the process of installing drivers through the previous chapter.

Solution: Ensure a Functioning Arduino

Your computer may not detect the device if it doesn't have any power. Verify if the board itself is receiving electricity by looking at its LED. If it's not working, then the system is probably not getting any electricity. Check the power supply source and see if it's working.

If you have a board with dual power option, see if the jumper is set to receive electricity from your desired source. For instance, if you're using USB to power your board, look if the jumper is directed towards the USB side, which means the system should get power from this source. If not, disconnect the device first, set the jumper to the power source, and plug it again. Check if the LED indicator turns on to see if it will start working.

Solution: Reset the Device

An Arduino board has a reset device, which will be useful in loading problems while transferring codes. Reset the board using the reset button. Press and reset it for several seconds. After the waiting time, reload the program and see if it's working.

Solution: Diagnose USB Connection Problem

Most of the time, the hardware connection itself is causing the inconsistency. Code transfer won't be completed if the data pathway itself is busted. Solve this problem by changing your USB cable. There are several ways in diagnosing whether the cable is the problem. If you plug the board to your computer and it doesn't seem to detect it, try connecting using a different cable. Through the Arduino program, check if the serial port that should be assigned on your board is present or not.

Arduino Software is Not Working

Programs tend to not work as expected. An Arduino software that doesn't load properly is probably installed using a wrong or outdated program version than what the operating system requires. Usually, software incompatibility issues should render you unable to install the program to your computer. In this case, uninstall the program, download the newer version of the compatible installer then reinstall.

Another reason is the probability is you're using a third party Arduino program. Third party Arduino programs should work properly as promoted by Arduino developers. Uninstall your current program and download a new installer from the third party developer's official website. Don't download a file from other sources. Extract the file and install.

If the aforementioned solution failed, download the actual Arduino program. Install then see if the program will load.

Arduino Software is Freezing and Crashing

A freezing Arduino software is caused by program inconsistency. The conflicting program can be a process installed with a computer peripheral, driver or other files. Diagnose probable conflicting program using MSConfig. Load this utility and disable Startup programs and services. Restart your computer and load Arduino software. If Arduino program loaded flawlessly, there's a chance that one of your startup program is causing the issue. Try and test each program and service to identify the cause. Remember the result because you will need to end the process first before loading Arduino software to prevent lagging.

In some cases, the program is running slowly although it doesn't freeze or crash. This is also probably caused by some devices installed in your computer. A typical culprit is an installed of the COM port meddling with the loading process. Use MSConfig again to disable and diagnose program causes. Turn off your computer then unplug all the other devices in your computer. Turn the computer on then plug the device. Load the program and see if it's responding properly.

Chapter 6. Additional Tips and Tricks

Additional tips and tricks in using Arduino are always helpful for beginners. Take note of the following ideas to maximize your experience in using this PCB:

Don't Throw Damaged Arduino

The chances of damaging an Arduino PCB q43 are high for beginners. Don't worry because it happens as part of the learning process.

In case you damage a board, don't throw it away. You can still use it in getting familiarized with its parts. Dismantle its parts if you want to have an idea how each piece is installed. Doing so will be helpful once you're ready to create your custom board.

Save RAM through Coding

Writing a code saves the data in two locations: in the RAM and program memory. Program memory saves all the information while RAM deletes them once power supply in the board is interrupted. Activating the board requires RAM to copy the usual strings from the program memory. Therefore, you're using more resources that may slow down your project.

A good example of code that saves memory is Serial.println(F("Text to insert")); instead of writing it as Serial.println("Text to insert"). The former will draw out the text from the program memory via temporary buffer. No need for RAM to copy and load the data, which saves memory resources.

Take Note of Extra or Missing Code Characters

Make sure that the code you type doesn't have extra character. An additional character will keep the system from generating desired functions or results. Double check the code and remove extra characters.

The same goes for missing characters. Be sure to place semicolon on codes because it's a mandatory symbol.

Take Advantage of *Serial.list()* Command

Arduino program must read the board from the right port. You will know the available ports in your computer by typing *Serial.list()*. This command will list down all available ports for your board.

Add Notes on the Codes if Necessary

Writing notes on your codes is a good practice. You'll remember what the code is for or the result it should generate. Add a note beside a code line by setting a space then two slashes (//) then type your notes. For example:

```
int pin = 14

void setup()

{

 pin = 15

 pinMode(pin, OUTPUT); // Note 1 here.

}

void loop()

{

 digitalWrite(pin, High) // Note 2 here.

}
```

The slashes are an indicator that the next characters are not part of the code. The system won't interpret the characters and meddle with the results.

Take Precautionary Measures before Assembling

Although you're doing a simply project, Arduino installation requires safe handling. Soldering can burn and wound your fingers or hands. A drop of melted lead can also be painful on your skin. Follow soldering and building guides accordingly to keep you from accidents.

Start with the Following Projects

Start playing with Arduino hardware and software by doing the following simple projects. Follow the links to see the procedures and detailed list of needed parts:

- An e-dice using Arduino Uno
- A basic stopwatch
- A bar graph display
- A garage door opener
- An Arduino Drone (Italian)
- Thermostat

Conclusion

Thank you again for downloading this book!

I hope this book was able to help you to be familiarized with Arduino and its advantages to non-technology experts and hobbyists who want to build their own tech systems at home.

The next step is to do some recommended projects and learn proper handling and installation process for Arduino. Hone your skills and challenge yourself to bigger projects using Arduinos with higher specs.

Finally, if you enjoyed this book, then I'd like to ask you for a favor, would you be kind enough to leave a review for this book on Amazon? It'd be greatly appreciated!

Click here to leave a review for this book on Amazon!

Thank you and good luck!

Your Free Bonus

Windows 10: Top Tips and Tricks

Complete Updated Guide for Beginners 2015

Table of Contents

Introduction

Chapter 1 – A Look Inside the New Windows 10

Chapter 2 – How to Set Up Windows 10

Chapter 3 – Useful Tips and Tricks for Windows 10 Users

Conclusion

Introduction

The Windows operating system has been around for years and, despite all the updates, the interface has always been somewhat similar. Windows users have had no problems using the OS over the years. However, with the introduction of the Windows 8, a radical change occurred. The iconic Start menu was nowhere to be seen and the desktop was replaced by tiled-based system. This extreme change saw a lot of unfavorable feedback from users who were not happy. Thus, Microsoft caved in and gave the users what they wanted through the Windows 10.

The Windows 10 marked the return of the operating system that every Microsoft user knew and adored. The Start menu was brought back and the tiled-based system, while still present, is now integrated into the menu for easier viewing. Furthermore, Windows 10 also includes a voice-powered personal assistant, similar to Apple's Siri, known as "Cortana". You can ask 'her' about the date today, how the weather is and you can even ask for a joke. Finally, Microsoft has also eliminated the Internet Explorer and presented the new Microsoft Edge. This browser is more stylish and allows you to create reading lists and annotate web pages.

This book serves as your comprehensive guide to using the all-new Windows 10. In here, you will find the basics of navigating through the OS as well as tips and tricks for a smooth-sailing user experience.

Chapter 1: A Look Inside the New Windows 10

2015 incidentally marks the 30th year since Microsoft Windows was first commercially released. Since the first time it was launched, it has had several modifications and improvements but always the same satisfaction for its users. For its latest release, Windows 10, Microsoft guarantees excellent user experience for all their devices by bringing back old favorites and launching new features. Below are some of the essentials that you should familiarize yourself with.

1.1   Desktop

For the first versions of Windows, we were presented with a desktop that would soon become a classic sight – a background space, usually with a nature-themed wallpaper, filled with icons. When Windows 8 was brought in, it moved its attention away from the desktop, much to the dismay of Windows users. But with the all-new Windows 10, the desktop was once again the center of PC interaction. Just like old times, users can customize the desktop with wallpapers and add shortcuts. The taskbar is also in the bottom of the screen. However, unlike the previous versions, the apps are windowed and resizable for a more versatile usage. The Windows 10 also introduces the Virtual Desktops. Generally, this feature allows you to add windows and applications into active desktops or open new ones by clicking the Task View button, thereby enabling you to widen your workspace and increase productivity.

1.2   Start Menu

When Microsoft removed the Start menu and replaced it with the Start screen for Windows 8, they received a lot of backlash from experienced Windows users. With Windows 10, the developers brought back the Start menu, but with a few tweaks. It finds itself back in its original spot at the bottom left corner of the taskbar. In its default settings, the new Start menu has Windows 8's Live Tiles along with the usual desktop apps and places. But users now have the option to turn off the Live Tile feature and unpin the Metro Apps. On the other hand, they can also choose to view the menu in full screen. All in all, customization is flexible to cater to the users' preferences, whether they want the old-school or more modern style of operation. The interface basically has these four features:

- **Start Menu** – the left area pins the applications, primarily the most-used ones, popular system locations and places.

- **Search Bar** – allows users to look for documents, folders and applications and allows you to directly run the apps.

- **Live Tiles** – the right area pins Metro apps, which can be rearranged simply by clicking and dragging.

- **Power Button** – located at the top of the menu and has Sleep, Restart and Shut Down options.

1.3 Microsoft Edge

The Microsoft Edge, which was initially codenamed as "Project Spartan", is the newest default web browser for the Windows 10 OS. It was first unveiled in January 2015 and is meant to be the successor of the now-obsolete Internet Explorer. The Edge is faster and more innovative than its predecessor: it let users share annotated pages using Web notes and features a "Hub" panel which collects history, downloads, reading lists and favorites. In addition, it can be integrated with Cortana, allowing for easier searching.

1.4 Cortana

Thanks to smartphone technology, voice operation has become more advanced. Cortana, which was initially launched as a feature of the Windows Phone 8.1, is Microsoft's smart personal assistant that responds either to voice or typed commands and rivals Apple's Siri. Now a part of the Windows OS for desktop, Cortana can be accessed via the "Hey Cortana" command or taskbar search bar. It can carry out tasks such as searching for folders, files or applications, sending e-mails and reminding events on calendar. It also utilizes Bing search technology, making it easier for users to perform web searches or look for sports scores, weather reports and the like. When you use Cortana this way often, "she" becomes aware of your interests, working habits, quiet times and favored locations. It also has settings where you can do vocal training and ask Cortana to call you by your name. If you are not fond of using Cortana, you have the option to turn it off altogether. This feature really feels like you have your own personal assistant.

1.5 Windows Hello

This is Windows 10's latest login system extending Microsoft Passport, elevating Windows security. With Windows Hello, users are given an exclusive four-digit pin for a universal login. Login can also be achieved through physical features recognition such as fingerprint sensor and IR camera. These peripherals enable the users to scan fingerprints, face and iris. These biometric data are not only used for login purposes; they can also be used to perform other functions such as buying from the Windows Store.

1.6 Windows Store

The Windows Store was first introduced with Windows 8 as a way to download and install applications on the PC and other devices. The Windows 10 version involved a few changes and improvements. The new Beta facelift is more accessible and has a new design. The primary layout of the "Home" page is more organized and presents a myriad of featured and latest applications at the top area. It also shows download queues, search bar, account profile and links to core Apps, Music, TV and Games categories. Scrolling through the Store is now done vertically, which is easier compared to the horizontal scrolling from the previous interface, making it way easier to browse through. All these simple but insightful tweaks are delightfully welcomed by Windows users.

1.7   File Explorer

For the longest time, browsing the contents of Windows PCs is mainly done through the Windows Explorer. This tradition remains with Windows 10. However, it is now called the File Explorer. With this feature, PC users can browse local folders as well as network places, connected drives and the OneDrive cloud storage. In essence, it still has the original window on the left side that exhibits the folder trees and the right side which previews thumbnails. But one noticeable difference is the "Quick Access" view, wherein you can find items shown in modifiable smart categories. The groupings of files and folders are tagged as "Recent files", "Favorites" and "Frequent folders", which makes for easier location and navigation. Just like most features of Windows 10, the Folder Options can be modified according to your preferences through View>Options.

1.8   Action Center

The Action Center, similar to Cortana, was also originally a feature of the Windows Phone. Making its leap from phone to Windows 10, this feature is where notifications can be viewed. Lodged in a fly-out panel on the right area of the desktop, the Action Center stores real-time notifications from important events. In here, you can check applications, communication and system events live. To dismiss and remove the notifications, you simply need to click the "X" button. Another feature, "Windows everywhere" makes it possible for users to sync the experience over multiple Windows devices such as tablets, PCs and phones.

1.9   Settings

Every veteran Windows user knows that the most significant settings of the operating system can be discovered in the Control Panel. While the Control Panel is still present in the Windows 10 OS, it is placed within the new "Settings" app, which is located on the left side of the Start menu. The app presents a more modernized and efficient view where icons for Devices, System and Network & internet can be found. Aside from the preferences for Wi-Fi, displays, peripherals and power management, PC users can also personalize the looks, accessibility and privacy levels of Windows 10. What's more, the design of the Settings app is universal for all Windows devices. To get to more advanced options in the Control Panel, users may utilize the search bar located on the top right corner. Generally, there are four main aspects:

- Personalization and Accounts – lets users set options for how they want their system to look as well as managing the system accounts

- System and Devices – vital settings for the present Windows 10 system as well as any peripherals or devices connected

- Settings search – uses the Search bar to look for a particular setting that you cannot find via navigation

- Update and Recovery – where crucial options for keeping Windows 10 up to date can be found

Chapter 2: How to Set Up Windows 10

Now that you know what Windows 10 has to offer, it is now time to learn how to set it up on your PC. Here are the essential procedures that you need to know:

2.1   Installing Windows 10

There are a number of ways to install Windows 10 in your computer. However, in this guide, we will only be tackling two of the most common methods – upgrading from an older version and using an installation media.

How to upgrade from Windows 7 or 8

Upgrading your current Windows 7 or 8 to Windows 10 is actually very simple. If your OS is up to date, then you will be able to spot a Windows icon at the right side of your task bar. Clicking that icon will take you to the Get Windows 10 app, which will then check your computer's compatibility and enable you to sign up for a download of the new OS. Once this is done, you can simply enter your e-mail address and wait for the update to take place.

If the Windows icon does not appear, it means that you need to make some updates first. For Windows 7 users, your OS needs to be updated to Service Pack 1. To do so, you need to open the Start menu and do a search for Windows Update. Click the "Check for Updates" button and install the update. For Windows 8 users, you will need to have the 8.1 version to upgrade to Windows 10. To do this, go the Store tile found on the Start screen. In here, you will find the icon for the update. Once your computer has the latest version of either Windows 7 or 8, you should be able to see the Get Windows 10 app icon on the taskbar and get the free upgrade.

How to install Windows 10 using installation media

For users who want to do a clean install, they will have to create Windows 10 installation media using either a USB Flash Drive with at least 4GB free storage or a blank DVD and a burner. Take note that all your files will be erased so make sure you back up all your date before you proceed with the installation. Here are the steps you need to follow:

a. Download the media creation tool from the Microsoft website. There are 2 versions – 32-bit and 64-bit. Choosing the right version is dependent on which system you are using it on. Typically, 32-bit versions are the better option because not all computers are 64-bit capable. To be safe, you may download both. Only the one compatible with your system would work.

b. Run the tool that you have downloaded. Choose the "Create installation media for another PC" option and click the "Next" button.

c. Choose the Language, Edition and Architecture options compatible with your system and click Next.

d. Choose which media to use, either a USB flash drive or DVD. The former is easier and more advisable because it works in all computers as opposed to the latter, which requires a CD slot and burner.

e. If you choose the flash drive option, you then have to select your USB from the list of available drives. Your download will now start. The time needed for download varies depending on the speed of your Internet connection. If you choose the DVD option, you will have to burn the downloaded file onto the blank DVD. Restart your computer.

f. Insert your installation media on the computer that you want to upgrade to Windows 10. Open the drive in Windows Explorer and click on the Setup file. This will start the upgrading process.

g. Your computer will check updates and ask to agree to the terms and conditions. Once this is done with, a "Ready to Install" dialog box. Click on the "Change what to keep" option.

h. Here, you may pick "Nothing" (which will reset everything), "Keep personal files, apps or Windows settings" (which is not a clean installation and will only give you a Windows 10 upgrade) or "Keep personal files only" (which will retain your photos, documents, music, etc.). Once you have chosen, click on "Next".

i. Follow the rest of the steps of the installation.

There you have it! After you execute these steps, you will now have Windows 10 up and running on your computer.

2.2   How to create Microsoft and user accounts

Creating a Microsoft account

The Windows 10 features two kinds of user accounts: a Microsoft account and a local one. Local accounts, similar to those from older OS such as Vista and Windows 7, include a username and password in order to log in to the computer. The details are stored and there is no need to connect to the Internet. If you upgraded your OS from Windows 7, chances are that your user account for Windows 10 is local. Having a Microsoft account gives users access to special features that are not available to people with local accounts such as Outlook e-mail address, OneDrive online storage, Windows Store and Office web apps and similar settings on various computers. As the versions of Windows keep changing, it keeps getting harder to use the OS without a Microsoft account. If you install Windows 10 on your PC, you will be asked to create a Microsoft account. To do this, here are the steps you need to follow:

a. Upon sign in, the page will ask you to enter your e-mail address and password. If you have a previous Microsoft account, you simply need to fill in the boxes. Otherwise, click on the "Create one" link.

b. Enter your name and the e-mail address that you are currently using. If you want a new e-mail address, click on the "Get a new e-mail address" link, which will enable you to create your own Outlook account.

c. Enter the desired name for your outlook.com address in the box.

d. Enter the password that you will be using for your Microsoft account. To make sure it is not easy to figure out, it must be at least 8 characters.

e. Enter your phone number. This is useful in case you have problems with the account.

f. A link found at the bottom part lets you add another active e-mail address as backup. Fill this up if you want.

Once all the fields have been filled up, you now have a Microsoft account that you can use on any device.

Creating a user account

For shared computers at home, Windows has an option to make separate accounts for its users. There are quite a few reasons why users would want individual accounts. Each user gets to have his or her personal folders, documents and data. Additionally, parents can set restrictions on the accounts of their children. What sets the user accounts of Windows 10 is that all users are required to have an e-mail account to be able to log in, which is a part of Microsoft's efforts to strengthen its security system. To set up a new user account, perform the following steps:

a. Click the Start menu and go to Settings.

b. In the Settings window, choose Accounts.

c. Choose the "Family & other users". On the right side, you can add a person or a family member.

d. Whether it is for adults, children or other users, adding works the same way. You have to either add the users' e-mail addresses or click on the link below. This link will enable you to create one.

e. Once the e-mail address/es have been entered, an invitation will be sent to the owner.

f. On the main screen, you will see that the user/s you have added will show up as something like this: "Adult, Pending". This means that the e-mail address is awaiting confirmation from the owner.

g. To confirm and become a new user, the owner of the e-mail must log in their account and go to the Mail app. In their inbox, they will find an "Accept Invitation" link, which they then have to click to complete the process.

It is important to note that, while the adult and child accounts are created in similar fashion, they vary when it comes to capacities. Adult accounts can restrict child accounts, such as software and Internet usage, through the Windows Parental Controls.

2.3 Setting up Windows Firewall and Windows Defender

How to set up Windows Firewall

Each latest Windows release comes with an improved security. Unfortunately, despite the boost, there are still hackers and malware that can wiggle their way into the computer to leave a virus or gather files. Hence, users should try to take measures to prevent any security threats. One way to improve computer security is through a firewall. This is meant to thwart unauthorized users and software from getting into your system. Windows Firewall jams incoming connections from both the local network and Internet without interrupting the normal operation of software in your computer. It is also highly valuable in preventing third-party invaders whenever you connect to a public Wi-Fi network. More often than not, Windows Firewall is activated by default. However, there are instances wherein users have to enable it manually. To do so, execute the following steps:

a. Look for the location of the firewall by browsing through Settings or doing a quick search in the search bar. Click on "Check firewall status" or Windows Firewall from the results.

b. If the Firewall is turned off, a quick fix would be to click the button that says "Use Recommended Settings".

c. Click the "Turn Windows Firewall on or off" link on the left side. You will be redirected to a screen which has options for turning Windows Firewall on for private and public networks. Choose your preferred options, although it is advisable to at least turn on the firewall for public network. In addition, tick the boxes for notifications.

d. You should be able to see green check icons, which indicate that your Windows Firewall is up and running.

How to set up Windows Defender

Even if Windows 10 has enhanced security compared to its predecessors, extra precautions should still be taken to block adware, malware and spyware. One security program offered by Microsoft upon installation is the Windows Defender. Although it is not as superior as other third-party anti-virus programs, the Windows Defender offers the computer real-time protection. It checks for any malware from downloads and other files saved on the disk and searches for any problem that the computer might have (e.g. malicious programs) and notifies users. To enable Windows Defender and to get it to scan your computer, you need to follow these steps:

a. Open the Start menu and click on Settings. Go to "Update & Security" and choose "Windows Defender". Be sure that all the options are turned on.

b. Look for Windows Defender going to the Start menu and clicking "All Apps". In the W section, choose "Windows System" and click on "Windows Defender".

c. The Windows Defender window should appear with three tabs on top and three scan choices on the right side. A green check mark indicates that things are okay.

d. Since the Windows Defender utilizes a virus definitions database that is regularly updated, you need to ensure that you have the latest version. You can do this by going to the Update tab and clicking on "Update".

e. To scan your computer for any malware, go to the Home tab and click "Scan now". It is advised that quick scans are conducted every day while full scans are done every week.

f. After scanning, the green check mark should appear, meaning there are no threats detected. If any malware was found, it will be erased.

While the Windows Defender is effective in its own right, it is still ideal to have another anti-virus program (e.g. AVG, Bitdefender) installed in your computer to ensure maximum protection.

These are the essential aspects of Windows 10 that you need to set up in your computer. Once you have followed these steps, your PC will now be ready for use.

Chapter 3: Useful Tips and Tricks for Windows 10 Users

Windows 10 may be Microsoft's best operating system yet. Despite the fact that it was just recently launched, it is already full of neat features that will excite any Windows user. But because of the major overhaul, some users find it difficult and confusing to use Windows 10. Hereunder are some of the most useful tips and tricks that you should know to ease the transition and ensure the best user experience.

3.1   How to master and customize the Start menu

For the longest time, the Start menu has been the single most important button in any Windows system. It has all the applications conveniently located in one area, making it easy for users to access whatever file, folder or program that they need. Therefore, when the Windows 8 came out and the beloved Start menu was removed, users were outraged. While the live screen was effective for touch devices, it was not favorable for the traditional computer with keyboard and mouse. So, with the reintroduction of the Windows 10 is the return of the Start menu, albeit with a few upgrades.

Getting to know the Start menu

The Start menu can be found in its original spot in the lower left side of the screen. Upon opening the menu, you will find the customary functions (e.g. Programs, File Explorer, Settings) on the left side. The user name located on top connects to the user's Microsoft accounts such as OneDrive. You will find live tiles that display programs and relevant information on the right side. The applications are also organized in alphabetical order, making it easier to find which program you want to open. There is also a search bar located at the bottom of the menu, which can be used to locally detect programs and files as well as searching the Internet for related information. There is also a Cortana button specifically designed to open the voice control.

Start menu customization

Apart from the new interface, Windows 10's version of the Start menu is also fully customizable and can be tailored according to the user's preferences. Here are some of the key changes that you can make on the Start menu as well as its applications:

- **Unpin or resize an icon** – in the Start menu, right-click on an icon. This will prompt a drop-down list where you can choose whether to unpin or resize.

- **Moving icons** – to change the position of an icon, simply drag and drop it to desired spot.

- **Live tiles** – you can switch live content on and off by right-clicking on the tile.

- **Change color theme** – Click on "Choose a color" and pick out preferred color from the panel.

- **Customize list** – in the left-hand column, click on Settings and choose "Customize list". This will enable you to pick which shortcuts will show up.

- **Show a full menu** – in Settings, look for "Use full-screen Start when in the desktop" option and enable it. This will display the Start menu above all other elements.

- **Access extra settings** – while on desktop, right-click anywhere and choose "Personalize", which will bring up an entire panel of additional customization settings for the Start menu.

These are some of the primary changes that are available to your Start menu. There are some that were not covered that can be easily discovered upon further use. Once you get the hang of it, customizing the Start menu should be a breeze!

3.2   How to use virtual desktops

Windows 10 has finally jumped on the bandwagon and made virtual desktops a central part of the system. In essence, it is like having full row of desktops located side by side. However, you can only see one desktop at a time. A vital feature of the virtual desktop is you can move sideways from one desktop to another and drag and drop them wherever you desire. In general, the new virtual desktop is a better and more productive way of organizing your desktop activities. To maximize the use of the virtual desktop, here are the basic tricks you need to know:

- **Open the Task View** – you can do this by clicking the taskbar icon found next the search bar or simply hit the Windows key + Tab.

- **Creating a new desktop** - when Task View comes up, you will have Desktops 1 and 2. On the lower-right part, click on "New Desktop" to create a new desktop.

- **Move apps from one desktop to another** - when moving applications, simply drag the app thumbnail to the thumbnail of the desktop where you want to move it.

- **Move apps to a new desktop** - If you want to move an application to a new desktop, you simply need to drag the app thumbnail to the "New

Desktop" button and Windows will automatically create the new desktop with the app in it.

- **Preview a desktop** - similar to the Alt + Tab feature of previous versions of Windows, the Task View enables a preview a certain desktop without having to switch to it. To do this, simply hover the mouse curser over the desktop and a preview of its contents will appear.

- **Customize virtual desktop settings** – to view all applications across every desktop in the Task View and taskbar, go to Start menu and click on Settings. Open System > Multi-tasking > Virtual desktops.

The virtual desktop is a superb way to spread out and group your applications according to your preference. Think of it as having a particular desktop for every need that you have.

3.3   How to use Cortana

By now, you already know that Cortana is Microsoft's smart personal assistant. Just like a real PA, you can speak to Cortana as if she is an actual person and she will respond. Users can use Cortana to search the web, set appointments and even tell jokes. Overall, it is a fun feature that also improves accessibility. The Cortana is featured in the search box located beside the Start button. To capitalize on the many features of Cortana, learn the following tricks:

- **How to activate Cortana**

Naturally, you will not be able to use Cortana if she is disabled. To activate, you need to:

a. Click the search box beside the Start button;

b. In the window that will pop up, click on the "I'm in" button. After reading the terms, click on "I agree".

c. On the next window, you have the option to turn on the "Hey, Cortana" feature, which allows you to use your voice to make commands without clicking anything. If you want this feature turned on, click the "Yes please" option.

d. On the last window, type in the name that you would like Cortana to address you with and click on the "Use that" button to confirm.

- **Use Cortana to search for information**

One of the many things that you can ask Cortana to do is run a search about practically anything under the sun. You may do this by either typing in the keyword on the search box or clicking the microphone icon and doing a voice command.

- **Get Cortana to know more about you**

Just like with an actual PA, Cortana will work at her best once she has more information about you. Windows 10 features a Notebook wherein all your interests are being recorded. This enables Cortana to yield more significant search results. To record in the Notebook, you need to follow these three simple steps:

a. Click the search box located beside the Start menu.

b. In the sidebar, click on the "Notebook" icon.

c. Go through each category that appears and pick out your preferences. Every category you choose will cause subcategories to show up.

Once you have selected the categories that you are interested in, Cortana will use it as reference when carrying out searches.

- **Enabling "Hey, Cortana" feature**

This is for the users who might have disregarded enabling the "Hey, Cortana" feature during the initial activation. Likewise, it also allows users to turn off the feature just in case. To enable "Hey, Cortana", follow these steps:

a. Click on the search box beside the Start button.

b. Click the Notebook icon within Cortana's window.

c. Click on Settings.

d. A Settings window will appear. Switch the "Hey, Cortana" option to ON.

Once the switch is turned to ON, you can now use the function by simply saying "Hey, Cortana" and then speaking your command.

The abovementioned tips can help you take full advantage of Windows 10's Cortana and make your work easier.

3.4   Mastering Microsoft Edge

Microsoft Edge is the newest web browser offered in Windows 10 and technically replaces the original Internet Explorer. The browser is much faster and has a lot to offer. Below are some of the necessary tricks that you should know to capitalize on Windows' latest browser.

- **Share web pages**

Sharing web pages has become easier thanks to the integrated Share button found on the Edge toolbar. To do this, simply click on this button, which will open a system panel. Choose where you want to share the web page from the list of apps. You can add to this list by downloading sharing-supported apps from the Store. For instance, if you want to share pages on Facebook, you will have to get the app and install it on your computer. Another neat trick would be to tap the page title in the Share panel and share a screenshot of the web page as opposed to sending a link.

- **How to change to Reading View mode**

Edge, along with most modern browsers, features a "Reading View" function. As its name suggests, this feature removes any clutter from web pages and converts the page into a version that is easier to read. To activate this mode, simply click on the "reading view" icon located in the address bar.

- **Managing the Reading List**

Also new in the Microsoft Edge is its reading list feature. This is for pages and articles you want to read at a later time. It is stored separately from your saved Favorites. To add a page to your reading list, click on the star icon found in the address bar and choose the "Reading list" heading. This will add the page to your current reading list.

To manage your reading list, click on the "hub" button and choose the "Reading List" category. Your saved pages will show up and you will then be able to access them.

- **Add annotations to your page**

Perhaps what sets the Microsoft Edge apart from other browsers is its annotation features, which is the primary reason why it is said to be the premier browser for "doing". To annotate a web page, click on the "Make a Web Note" button on the toolbar. Make use of the tools available to add notes, copy, draw on, erase and highlight parts of the page. Click on the "Save" button to save the annotated page to your Reading List, Favourites or on Microsoft OneNote. You also have the option to share it on other apps through the Share button.

- **Switch to dark theme**

There are some users who prefer darker shades over the lighter default theme. Luckily for them, Windows offers a dark theme. To switch, open menu from the toolbar and click on "Choose a theme". Pick the "Dark" option to activate the dark theme.

- **Enable Private Browsing**

Edge's InPrivate allows users to surf the web without leaving any history data, similar to Chrome's incognito mode. To enable this feature, go to the menu located in the toolbar and click on "New InPrivate window". This will open up a new window for private browsing.

- **Pin pages to Start menu**

The Edge browser enables users to easily pin pages to the Start menu. To do this, open the menu and simply choose the "Pin to Start". This will pin the current page as a tile to the Start menu or Start screen. In doing so, users can gain instant access to the pinned page with just a click of the mouse.

3.5   Purchase apps from the Windows Store

Microsoft's latest OS now features a Windows Store, where all the apps can be found. In here, apps are brilliantly categorized and easy to browse. Similar to the format in the mobile version of Windows, programs are no longer installed individually; rather, the apps are now available for download and purchase through the Store. To newbies who are not yet familiar with the Windows Store, here are the procedures when buying an app:

a. The first step is to find the app that you want to purchase. There are two ways to do it. The first way to do it is to launch the Windows Store and click on "App categories". Look for the category that your app falls under and browse until you find it. The second and easier way to do it is to simply use the Search bar located at the top of the Store and type in the name or keyword of the app you are looking for.

b. After finding the app, click on the thumbnail and you will be directed to a page. Click on "More" to read user reviews and other additional information about the app. You can let others know about the app by clicking on the "Share" icon and choosing which platform you want to share it in.

c. For free apps, simply click on the "Free" button and the download will start. For paid apps, click on the icon with the price in it. This will prompt you to log in to your Microsoft account and will ask for payment confirmation. Once confirmed, the download will initiate.

d. To manage your downloads, click the account icon at the upper right hand of the screen and select "Downloads". From here, you can manage your downloaded apps. You will also find a "Check for updates" option, which informs you if there are new fixes or features for your current apps.

The Windows Store is fairly easy to understand, especially since its format is similar to many app stores on other devices. It also boasts of a vast selection of apps falling under a wide range of categories such as films, music, games, education, business and books, among others.

3.6 Essential keyboard shortcuts

Keyboard shortcuts make navigation easier and can improve workflow. For Windows 10 users, here are some of the most important and practical keyboard shortcuts:

- **Windows Key + Tab** = Opens Task View

- **Windows Key + CTRL + Left or Right Arrow** = Switches virtual desktop

- **Windows Key + Left or Right Arrow** = Window snapping

- **Windows Key + Up or Down Arrow** = Snaps windows to top or bottom of screen

- **Windows Key + CTRL + C** = Activates Cortana listening

- **Windows Key + CTRL + D** = Opens new virtual desktop

- **Windows Key + CTRL + F4** = Closes active virtual desktop

- **ALT + Tab** = Switch to recent window

- **Windows Key + S** = Daily Glance for news, weather and sports

3.7 Enable Battery Saver

For laptop users, there is a Battery Saver option to end background services and other programs when the battery is dangerously close to running out. To enable this feature, go the Start Menu and click on Settings > System > Battery Saver.

Conclusion

I would like to thank you for downloading this book! This marks the end of your journey through this Windows 10 guide.

The Windows 10 operating system is, without a doubt, the best one that Microsoft has launched in the recent years. It is a perfect mix of the classic Microsoft system we all know and the modernized version that was first introduced in Windows 8. It is sleek, revolutionary and innovative.

It may be daunting to use at first because of the many changes that comes with the upgrade. This book is meant to serve as your handbook to getting around Windows 10 and understanding how the new system works. It aims to show the readers what to expect and details key steps and procedures to make the Windows 10 experience fun and easy.

I sincerely hope the information found in this book was of immense help to you. Now, the next thing for you to do is to take what you have learned and apply it when using your Windows 10 computer. Best of luck!

Preview Of 'Insert Book Title Here'

This section is designed to provide the reader a preview of one of your other books. Simply copy and paste a chapter of another book that you have available on Kindle and link to it below.

Click here to check out the rest of (insert book name here) on Amazon.

Or go to: **http://www.mybitlylink.com** (insert shortened bit.ly link)